HOW TO LOVE YOURSELF

LIKE THERE WERE NO TOMORROW

MATT MORRIS

HOW TO LOVE YOURSELF

Like There Were No Tomorrow

Matt Morris, CPCC

INTRODUCTION

Who Are You?

If you have been feeling down in the dumps and have given up all hopes in life, just ask one question to that self within you: "Who am I?" Is it you that has failed or it's just the circumstances that have come between you and your success? The first option is not possible because if it was you that had failed, then who was that person who has seen good times earlier and even tasted success? If you could succeed then, if you could conquer the challenges you had to face earlier and if you were happy and contented sometime back; then it's definitely not you that has filed. No person can be 100% failure.

You have the ability to succeed. You have proved it earlier. Then what has happened now? The answer is the second option...the unfavorable circumstances surrounding you have failed you. They have forced you to give up. It's these circumstances that have managed to overpower your confidence and abilities and labeled you a "failure". But, for how long these circumstances will continue to overpower you and your willpower? Look within yourself... search for that soul within you who is waiting for an opportunity to dethrone the circumstances that have taken hold of your life and emerge successful.

But, the only person who can give that opportunity to your soul is yourself. And for this; you need to build confidence that you have lost. Start by searching for your true self and your true abilities that have been suppressed by the circumstances. I have identified 7 components that form the basic foundation of our life and personality. Let's take a closer look at them to learn, "Who are you?"

1. **The Core Connection**

Everything in our life begins from our core connection. This side of our personality is made up of the deeply held values, response patterns, beliefs and passions we have been taught and been following since childhood. This is the connection where your paradigms of pleasure and pain are born and reside. Analyze your personal perspectives of life based on these factors to learn your core identity.

1. **The Motive Connection**

Motive is the "why" part of your identity. This connection forms the base for the reasons of doing the things that you do. It's your personal "why" behind your every action and thought. Motive is also related to your understanding of the concepts of success and failure. Knowing why you took certain actions and what your motive behind them was will help you define the "success" you desired. For example; if you think your motive for working few extra hours for a week or two was to prepare for a presentation that could help you get the desired promotion; then getting the promotion is your success.

1. **The Vision Connection**

Vision is the driver of our true self. We all visualize ourselves in the context of where we are now and where we would like to be in the future. Our vision of our aim or goal in life is totally personalized because it is created by us based on our unique vantage point. Understand what is your long terms goal and where do you visualize yourself after few years. If you think you have failed in achieving the goals you had set earlier, be honest with yourself to understand whether the goals were realistic and what could have probably lead to the failure. Understanding and accepting the reasons for failure will help you work on them or avoid them in future.

1. **The Path Connection**

The course you choose to walk can have a powerful influence on where you end up. The path you have selected is the journey aspect of your true self. Ask yourself how well thought out the path was in terms of what you wanted to achieve and what you actually have. Remember, since you have the freedom to choose your path; you also have to assume the responsibility for where it leads you. If you think your path could be the reason for your failure, you have the choice to make appropriate corrections and get on the right path this time.

1. **The Power Connection**

This factor of your personality has to do with how well you are able to manage your personal resources like motivation, focus, self-talk and commitment. It has to do with whether and how much do you allow the opposing forces like fear, anxiety and jealousy to influence us. These resources, when combined, determine the horse power behind our success and true self.

1. **The Identity Connection**

How do you define yourself in terms of your abilities? Do you think you are capable of doing any task or you have always considered yourself incapable of doing anything? Do you approve of yourself or are discontented with your own self? Do you feel undeserving or you are comfortable with the idea of achieving success at an individual level? Answers to these questions will help you understand whether you have been underestimating yourself. To achieve success in life, confidence is must. Have faith in your abilities. If you think you are lacking, be prepared to learn new skills and upgrade yourself to boost your confidence. The success will follow.

1. **The Fulfillment Connection**

The satisfaction side of our self defines how happy we are in life. Some people never feel any sense of satisfaction with regard to their accomplishments irrespective of how impressive their performance has been. This is usually an indication that something is amiss. Recognize your success - past as well as present. If you have been successful in the past, you know you have the potential to succeed in future as well. Identifying your success will not only build your confidence; but also make you feel contended in life.

If these primary components of our foundation are not fully integrated, our life becomes vulnerable to collapse. The identity crisis within yourself can cause a lot of confusion between what you do and who you actually are as a person. Introspecting about these 7 vital connections will help you realize your True Self and analyze your failure with regards to its actual reasons. And once you have indentified these, your journey from failure to success will be much easier!!!

ONE
HOW TO DEVELOP AN ACCURATE SELF-PERCEPTION

An accurate self-perception is an essential component of success and self-improvement. If you are not aware of your strengths and weaknesses, you will not know the areas you need to work on or how you can leverage your assets to your advantage! Self-perception means being aware of who you are and what you're capable of. Your self-perception is not limited to just having a positive self-esteem. It also involves acknowledging your shortcomings, adjusting how you view your skills and recognizing your problem areas.

Adjusting your self-perception about your skills comes down to being honest with yourself. Recognizing your weak points can be tough and may even hurt your sentiments. But, it will help you to identify when you need to ask for help. Acknowledging your strengths is as important as accepting your weaknesses. It gives you the courage and confidence to assert yourself even though you feel you don't deserve. Here's how you can develop an accurate self-perception and make adjustments when your perceptions do not line up with the reality.

Step One: Identify Your Self-Image Fallacies

Usually, the self-perception problem occurs because our misconceptions and emotions lead us to believe in false conclusions. The logical fallacies can sneak in easily and alter how you perceive yourselves each time you face a negative feedback or experience. For example: "I screwed up, so I am a screw up", "I'm not good at this now, so I will never be" or "This person doesn't like me, so nobody likes me"...Most people have this all-or-none mentality, which lends itself to a low self-esteem. Failing at something can be discouraging, but it's not right to assume that the failure means you're not good enough.

It is easier to focus on the negative. Most of us are good at dwelling on our mistakes; but bad when it comes to remembering when we got it right. We forget that one negative can not eliminate the positive. Do not let one instance of failure to make you perceive yourself as an incapable person. In fact, such failures show us how to get better.

The all-or-none phenomenon also exists the other way round. There are people who think, "I've never had any complaints, so I must be good." Unfortunately, such kind of thinking only leads to overestimation of one's self and result in a disaster when faced with a challenging situation. The chances of falling into depression are higher when you have failed after having overconfidence in self. The fact is; those closest to us are usually not the objective reviewers of our talents. So, unless your skills have been put to a test in an arena devoid of prejudice or bias (such as a public performance or workplace), a lack of complaints doesn't prove your talent.

Step Two: Perform a Self-Assessment

The next step for adjusting your perception to reality is to identify how you see yourself. To get started, write ten of your strengths on one side of a paper and ten weaknesses on the other. This exercise will force you to take an honest look at yourself and develop your Self-Esteem Inventory. You may need to seek input from others if you can not come up with the tens for both the sides.

Once you have done this, you will be able to change some of the weaknesses by working on them. Start with one weakness at a time, preferably the one that you can get over in the shortest possible time with ease and without anyone's help. Once you have achieved this, you will start feeling better about yourself and also develop the confidence needed to work on the other difficult-to-overcome weaknesses. And remember, nobody can change overnight. It may take a longer than expected time for the results to come. So set realistic expectations for your goals.

Step Three: Seek Outside Input

Outside input has the ability to validate as well as negate how you perceive yourselves. If you think you're not that great of a singer, but if the crowd at a karaoke disagrees; you have a reason to change your opinion. So, seeking outside input is absolutely necessary when you are trying to adjust your self perception.

As it turns out, not everyone is completely forthright when you ask for an opinion (though usually for a good reason). Here are some tips on how to get an honest feedback.

- Read between the lines. Look for what they didn't say rather than what they did. This can take practice. When you are singing, check if the audience is really enjoying. If you gave a persuasive speech, did they just enjoy it or did it actually change their opinion?
- Some people need encouragement to give out

their honest opinion. Pull out the honesty gradually. You may need to coax them a bit to get their opinion. Make it clear that you are fine with the harshest of their remarks and give them an opportunity to reveal more.

And most importantly: once you get the feedback, accept it. The most common mistake made by people after getting feedback from others is filtering out the stuffs they don't like. "Oh! I can play the guitar just too well, they're just jealous" Right? Nope. When you asked for the feedback, be prepared to accept it even if it's uncomfortable. If it's true, you'll hear it from more than one person.

Step Four: Step Outside Your Comfort Zone to Challenge Yourself

Feedback from others is just one way to find out about your capabilities. It's a faster, reliable and a more effective way of getting a realistic picture of yourself. Having a realistic approach to what you can do, coupled with some optimism that things can turn in your favor if you worked hard at it, can be a key to making it happen. To put it simply, if you understand the risks; but still choose to be hopeful about the outcome, you can not only perform better, but also be happier and satisfied with the outcome.

Being realistic as well as optimistic can help you do better than the less grounded peers probably because you do not delude yourself into thinking you would do well without working hard. By evaluating your capabilities and the situation and then challenging yourself to fight the odds, you will be better equipped to handle the difficult circumstances in life.

Step Five: Emulate the Habits of Others

How you perceive yourself can also affect how you

behave. But, the relationship also works in the reverse. Something simple like faking a powerful body language can help you feel confident. This trick works well for most people. If you think you're too cynical, try being optimistic on social media even though you do not feel so. The idea is when you start hunting for the good, you may find it.

Our self-perception is instilled in us before we have a say in it. By indentifying your real self, you can find your hidden strengths and improve the weaknesses you never knew you had and get more successful in life.

TWO
HOW BEING UNHAPPY CAN AFFECT YOUR HEALTH

Depression and feeling unhappy have a strong link to several physical conditions. Being unhappy can make the pain, disability and distress from physical health problems more severe. Not feeling good about yourself and dwelling on a failure does not affect your confidence alone. It also impacts your health through the release of negative hormones, which produce a cascading effect on several functions of the body resulting in health complications.

ON THE CONTRARY, being happy improves your emotional health and makes you more aware of your thoughts, feelings and behaviors. It helps you learn and adopt the healthy ways of coping with the stress and challenges that are a normal part of life. However, sometimes certain things may happen in your life that can disrupt your emotional health. These things include:

- Being laid off from your job

- Dealing with the death of a loved one
- Strained personal relationships
- Suffering from an illness or an injury
- Experiencing financial losses

THESE "BAD" changes in life can lead to strong feelings of stress, sadness and anxiety that can have a serious negative impact on your health. Here are a few health issues that are very common in people who feel unhappy most of the time.

LIFESTYLE ISSUES

PEOPLE WHO ARE discontented are less likely to have a healthy lifestyle. They have a higher rate of smoking and lower exercise levels. They also have a tendency to ignore whether they are eating healthy food or not. This puts them at a higher risk of large number of chronic diseases like diabetes and even cancer. The risk of complications of these diseases is also higher in people who are unhappy and pessimistic than those who feel optimistic about recovering.

HYPERTENSION AND HEART **Attacks**

DATA SUGGEST THAT PEOPLE, who are anxious, stressed out and discontented, are at a higher risk of developing heart diseases like high blood pressure and heart attacks. The incidence as well as the severity of these illnesses is higher in such people. Feeling unhappy can also worsen the prognosis of a heart disease and increase the risk of death.

WEAK IMMUNE SYSTEM

POOR EMOTIONAL HEALTH can weaken the immune power of your body making you more prone to get infections during the emotionally difficult times. Besides, when you are feeling upset, stressed or anxious, you may not be in the right frame of mind to take good care of your health. You may not feel like eating nutritious foods, exercising or taking medicines your doctor has prescribed. This can lower your immunity further thereby increasing your likelihood of falling sick.

MENTAL DECLINE

DEPRESSION IS ASSOCIATED with a decline in the mental functioning. Being unhappy can affect your cognitive functions like memory, intelligence, attention span, concentration and the ability for logical reasoning. So, do not let the negative circumstances in your life to take hold of your emotions because it will also have an effect on your intellectual abilities making you less capable to fight back. Instead, be courageous and determined to find a way out as this will stimulate your brains to work harder to find a feasible solution to your problem.

. . .

CHANGES IN APPETITE

WHEN YOU ARE UNHAPPY, you either eat too much or too less. Either ways, it's going to be a bad news for your health. If you eat too much, you will gain weight that will put you at a risk of diabetes and hypertension. And if you lose weight, you will be left will too less energy to bounce back with new zest to face the challenges.

SLOW HEALING WOUNDS

RESEARCHERS HAVE FOUND that the local production of pro-inflammatory proteins called cytokines is lower in people who are stressed or unhappy. Due to this, the healing of wounds is delayed in these individuals.

DRUG ADDICTIONS

A STUDY HAS SHOWED that a large percentage of people addicted to drugs like cocaine had their first encounter with these poisonous substances when they were going through a rough phase in life. When a person is faced with a failure, he is more vulnerable to fall prey to drug addictions. The risk is more when he feels there is no way to get out of the situation and so, he tries to escape from the situation by taking the drugs that give him a "high". However, this "high" is temporary and lasts just for a few moments. It doesn't take the problem away from him. It's like closing the eyes and hoping the problem would just disappear. Sadly, that doesn't happen. The problem just worsens for you as you get addicted to higher and higher doses of the drugs, which gnaw into the healthy tissues of your body and make you a "sick" person! It would be wiser to say a big "NO" to these drugs when tempted to try one and rather concentrate on finding ways to solve the problems in life.

REDUCED SEX DRIVE

DEPRESSION and other negative emotions like feeling unhappy, stress, anxiety and fear have an ability to reduce your sex drive. As a result, it can also affect your personal relationships. Most men develop sexual difficulties like erectile dysfunctions and premature ejaculation. Stress can also lower the sperm count in men. These negative emotions also lower the sexual desire of a woman and cause a number of complaints like dry vagina, painful intercourse and infertility.

SLEEP DISTURBANCES

INSOMNIA (DIFFICULTY in falling asleep and staying asleep) is a major health problem of people who are always unhappy and dissatisfied with life. The inability to get sound sleep for at least 8 hours a day can have other serious consequences on the human body such as fatigue and low energy.

. . .

YOUR BODY RESPONDS to the way you feel and think. This is called the mind-body connection. When you are happy, your physical being also feels happy and stays healthy. Similarly, if you are feeling unhappy and do not feel motivated to fight back, your body, too, doesn't feel like fighting back for the survival. This results in the deterioration of your health. And this would be the last thing you would want to happen when you are already reeling under the pressure of negative circumstances. So, why dwell on what has already happened and complicate the matters? Learn to feel good even if the circumstances are contrary. This will trick your body into believing that everything is fine and this will give you the energy and stamina needed to fight back the challenge and emerge winner.

THREE
WHY LAUGHTER IS HEALTHY FOR YOU AND YOUR SUCCESS

Humor is infectious and we are happy about catching this infection. The sound of roaring laughter is more contagious than any sneeze, cough or sniffle. When laughter and smiles are shared, they bind people together and increase intimacy. Happiness can trigger healthy changes in your body. Laughter and humor boost your energy levels and protect you from the harmful effects of stress. And this is what you need when the tiredness – both mental as well as physical – and the stresses in life are out to push you deeper into a dark zone of hopelessness. Use this laughter and happiness to your advantage against the bad phase in your life to stay healthier, energetic and optimistic about the life and the outcome of your efforts. Here are some health benefits of bringing laughter and humor into your life that will also help you to conquer failure with a smile and embrace success.

Laugher brings good mood

Whether it is your personal life, career, business or social life, everything that you do depends on how good or bad your mood is. If your mood is good, you can do the things much better. Laughing and being happy changes the mood within seconds by releasing certain chemicals called endorphins from your nervous system. This helps you to remain cheerful and optimistic throughout the day and improves your physical productivity and mental abilities to work better.

Healthy exercise

Laughing works like an aerobic exercise. While laughing, there is no conscious thought process. All our senses effortlessly and naturally combine in a moment of harmony, to give peace, joy and relaxation. You can do this exercise anytime and you do not need to sweat out lifting heavy dumbbells for practicing this. It also brings more oxygen to the brain and lungs, which helps you to feel fresh and energetic. Laughter is the only exercise routine that reduces mental, emotional and physical stress simultaneously.

Strengthens immunity

It has been found that people who are generally happy are healthier and fall sick less often than those who have a tendency to be gloomy and sad. Laughter strengthens the immune system and prevents you from falling sick. It also helps in hastening the recovery in patients having wounds, ulcers and infections by stimulating the immune system to work more efficiently. Humor also has the ability to boost the levels of infection-fighting antibodies in your body.

Improved blood flow

A study was conducted to check the changes in the flow of blood in the arteries when people were shown comedies or intense drama. After the screening, it was found that the arteries of the people who watched the comedy had efficient expansion and contraction of the blood vessels resulting in a smooth flow of blood through the arteries. But the blood vessels in the group of people who watched the drama were tensed up, which resulted in the restriction of the blood flow. This study proves that being happy ensures smooth blood flow to the different organs like the brain and the extremities and protects you from stroke and PVD (Peripheral Vascular Disease).

Controlled blood sugar levels

Happiness has a beneficial effect on the blood sugar levels of patients with diabetes. People who feel happy and relaxed have a better control over their blood sugar levels while people who are stressed or anxious have a higher tendency for dangerous fluctuations in the sugar levels. That is why; laughing and being happy is considered highly therapeutic for diabetic patients.

Ensures sound sleep

Sleep is one aspect of our life that helps us to stay healthy and energetic by allowing the body and the mind enough time to recharge itself for carryout out the tasks on the next day. If you do not sleep well, your "battery" gets exhausted and you can not perform well the next day. Humor and happiness can keep the nerves in the body calm and relaxed and help you to get a sound sleep. If you are tensed or worried, you can not sleep well as the disturbing thoughts keep interfering with your sleep process. If you have been worried or feeling hopeless, try watching a humorous TV show or read a comedy book before going to bed. This will help you get a sound sleep and you will get up the next day with a fresh and positive outlook.

Anti-stress effect

Laughter is considered the most economical anti-stress measure. Laughter is also an effective muscle relaxant. Laughter expands the arteries and sends more blood to the muscles in the body. Even a short bout of laughter can help decrease the amount of stress hormones -epineprine and cortisol – produced in the body. It can be said to be a form of dynamic meditation, which brings instant relaxation.

Hypertension and heart disease

There are a number of causes for hypertension and heart diseases including heredity, smoking, obesity and excessive intake of fatty foods. However, stress is one of the major factors that can worsen the effect of the other causative factors and increase your risk of developing the diseases by multifold. Laughter helps to control blood pressure by reducing the release of stress hormones and brings relaxation. A drop of 10-20 mm of blood pressure is noticed in individuals after they participated in a 10-minute laughter session.

Similarly, if you are at a risk of developing a heart disease, happiness could be the best preventive medicine for you. Laughing brings about an improved blood circulation and oxygen supply to the heart muscles and prevents heart attacks.

Natural pain killer

Laughter boosts the levels of endorphins in the body, which act like natural pain killers. Endorphins released as a result of happiness and laughter help reduce the intensity of pain in patients suffering from spondylitis, arthritis and muscular spasms. Many patients have reported a reduced frequency of tension headaches and migraine during stress-free periods.

Alleviates asthma and bronchitis

Laughter is one of the best respiratory exercises for people suffering from bronchitis and asthma. It improves the oxygen levels in the blood and increases the lung capacity. Laughter works like the chest physiotherapy recommended by doctors to bring out mucous from the respiratory passages. The therapy involves blowing forcefully into an instrument. The therapeutic benefits of this therapy can be accomplished by laughing, that too, more easily and almost free of cost.

Happiness and humor have been correlated with better health. It is the key that can unlock your failure and open the doors of success for you. It helps you to feel bright and cheerful and brings to the surface all the suppressed positive emotions to give you a perspective that's motivating and encouraging. Best of all, this priceless medicine is free, easy to use and available to all. So, start using this wonder medicine from today itself to take one more step towards your goals.

FOUR

WHY IS IT IMPORTANT TO LOVE YOURSELF TO ACHIEVE SUCCESS?

When you are facing difficulties in life, you may start disliking yourself for what you are and what you have done. Many people have a tendency to blame their destiny when they can not achieve success. However, unless and until you love yourself, you will not be able to gather that confidence and charisma needed for being successful.

Yes, loving yourself is an integral part of your journey towards success. Well, you may think that loving yourself could mean being narcissistic. But, I find this funny, rather contradictory! A true self-love can never be narcissistic. If it is narcissism, it can't be love. Self-love is accepting yourself for what you are while narcissism is just selfishness. Self-love starts by giving love, care and attention to yourself so that you understand yourself and your abilities better and can face any challenge in life with confidence.

Love flourishes when we give it to others, but it always starts with 'me'. Ultimately, we are the only ones responsible for our life, choices, actions and the resulting outcomes. So, we have no right to be neglectful towards ourselves. The reasons stated below show that loving yourself is essential for achieving success.

When you love yourself, you accept who you are

When you know yourself perfectly well, you are aware of all your positive and negative sides and you accept them. Knowing yourself doesn't mean you be satisfied with all your traits. Loving yourself means recognizing your negative traits and working on them to improve yourself. When you love yourself, you realize that you are the only one in this entire universe with your unique traits, potentialities and qualities. If you have some negative traits, you also have some positive ones. This thinking gives a great sense of confidence. It gives you a "kick" to work towards overcoming your limitations. When you accept who you are, you do not feel the need to compare yourself to others. And this is the most inspiring feeling ever.

It gives you approval

We all love charismatic, compassionate and confident people. We look for inspiration in people who have been successful and want to follow them. We also dream of becoming like them. All of us have this subconscious desire. When people need to talk to someone, they usually address the person who seems strong and confident. And this strength and confidence come from self-love. When you love yourself, there will be many people who will look up to you, have faith in you and would entrust you with making important decisions. This happens because when you love yourself, you exude a charisma and compassion that makes people follow you and believe in you. In fact, people who love themselves are more likely to get a better job, promotion and more admirers. I think it's a crucial reason to love yourself.

You will avoid self-torture

A sense of shame is the worst feeling any person can experience. This is very common in people who are obese. They are always dissatisfied with their weight, even though they have an overall pleasant personality. They try numerous diets and lose so much weight that sometimes they are forced to see a doctor. It's a terrible, yet a very common, situation that shows lack of love for yourself resulting in self torture. Loving yourself will help you avoid being anxious or depressed and make you less inclined to self-torture and stresses.

When you love yourself, you look better

This one's simple. When you concentrate on your strong points instead of bothering about your imperfections; you start feeling better from within and that reflects on your skin and face. Your face looks much calm and relaxed. You actually start looking better and attractive when you love yourself regardless of your imperfections. After all, nobody on this earth is perfect. So, why bother about the imperfections within you? If you are obsessed with your short height, broad nose, thin lips or such small nuisances; you will not notice your beautiful eyes, lovely dimples and kind heart. But once you accept your flaws, you become more beautiful.

You will have a better family life

When you love yourself, you know what you deserve. You are aware of your weaknesses and understand that others may have a few. This helps you to accept others the way they are. This sets realistic expectations in relationships. You learn to treat others with respect and in return, are never ill-treated. And this is very important for a healthy family life and happier children also. Children always try to emulate their parents' manners, behavior and views. The ability to love ones' self and others is a crucial thing your kids should learn. But, it will not be possible if the parents do not display this ability. When you love yourself, you set a healthy example for your kids. A research has proved that a child's happiness and success are largely dependent on the experience he received during his childhood. That's why; it's important to love yourself first if you want to teach your child to love himself and be happy.

When you love yourself, the world around you changes

When you fall in love with yourself, everything around you becomes more beautiful and appealing. Self-love enables you to look at people and life from a positive perspective. This makes you a better person and improves your emotional, psychological and physical state.

Self-love is the love for yourself that is extended to other people. You must have heard the old saying that you can not love others if you do not love yourself. The flow of self-love occurs two-way - giving and receiving. When you give care and attention to yourself, you automatically start loving everything and everyone surrounding you. You emit positive vibrations, which attract people towards you. They feel good in your company. This helps you to win several brownie points based on which you can build a successful career, business and even personal relations. And would you believe, all this just starts with self-love!

FIVE
THE 14 KEY THINGS YOU NEED TO DO TO FEEL HAPPY AND LOVE YOURSELF

The most powerful relationship you can ever have is the relationship with your inner self. Loving yourself is the key to being successful in life. It directly affects your work, the quality of your relationships, your faith and also your future. Here are some proactive ways to discover your self-love and to leverage the benefits for a better and happier future.

1. **Make a list of things you like**

Self-care is an essential part of self-love. Self care means different things to different individuals. We often expect others to make us feel good by taking us out for dinner or by giving a gift. To love yourself, you need to do exactly those things that you expect others to do for you. Prepare a list of things that make you feel special. Treat yourself once in a while with what you like to do. Go to an art show, eat lunch somewhere nice, see a movie, go to a festival....Take yourself on a date often until you fall in love with yourself!

1. **Spend time on your own**

The only way you can truly know yourself is by spending some time with your own. And this means being alone, completely alone. Get off the dating site. Stop chatting. No Facebook. No Twitter. No phone. No email. Disconnect yourself completely from the world. Go on a walk, explore a new place on your own. Do something you really like to do... And whatever it is, do it by yourself. The time you give to yourself is essential for building up your sense of self. Schedule these "me" days regularly.

1. **Forgive yourself for the past**

Stop going over your past mistakes. Forgive yourself for hurting people, apologize sincerely if you can and mean what you say. Learn a lesson from your mistakes and move on. Make an effort to change the habits that caused you to make the mistake or you'll continue to be that person and may repeat the same mistake in future and therefore not like yourself.

1. **Move forward from the past hurts**

This can be quite challenging. But, sometimes it becomes important to accept the apology that you never received. If you don't do this, you'll never be able to move forward. You will keep pondering over it again and again as if you're holding onto a hot coal. You will only be burning yourself from within. Learn to let go. Forgive those who have hurt you – it's one of the most empowering things you can do for yourself.

1. **Filter out the negative thoughts**

If you get a negative thought, thank it for coming and then send it away. What you think and tell yourself is like a cycle; it can have an effect on everything – the way you feel, act and what you think next. If you let the negative thought to stay in your mind, it will convert into negative actions and invite more negative thoughts. The only person who has the power to control your thoughts is yourself.

1. **Be honest with yourself**

There is truth in every story of success and failure. At the end of the day, you can not hide the reality from yourself. You know the truth about what happened in your life. You were there. If the truth in the stories of your life hurts your esteem, then perhaps it's the time to have a hard, but honest, look at your realities and take efforts to change them. Unless and until you do this, your inner soul will keep haunting you and will not let you love yourself.

1. **Follow your passion**

What gets you really excited? If something gets you going and gives you an adrenalin rush – just do it! Quit all excuses. If you want something – go for it! Be in charge of your life and how you spend your time! Spend each moment with positivity and focus on the things that make you happy. Do not let anything to hold you back from your passion.

1. **Acknowledge yourself**

When you do a job well - whether small or big - acknowledge your accomplishment. Toot your own horn! Celebrate your achievements by admitting you did an amazing job. No one else will do it for you if you do not recognize your achievement! When you are satisfied with your work, make a note of it on a small chit. Keep an "I love you" jar and keep putting these chits in it. It will be the proof of your achievements and give you a reason to love yourself when you look back at it on a down day.

1. **Believe in yourself**

Stop ignoring what your gut instincts are telling you. Listen to your intuition and go with it. Trust yourself above anyone else. You are the best judge of your own actions. Stop going to others for their advice and opinions on you. Instead ask yourself what you feel and think about the situation and your reaction to it. That matters more than what others think about it. This belief in yourself will help you validate your actions as right or wrong so that you can take corrective steps that will make you a lovable person.

1. **Live with gratitude**

When you wake up each morning, be thankful that you're here. Be grateful to your destiny for the things you have. Learn to say, "Wow, I'm really fortunate to be me!" Allow only those things and people into your life that you're grateful for, can inspire you or add value to your life. In the same token, make an effort to not lose contact with the people you feel grateful for. If you meet the person who's impacted you positively, tell him you would love to keep in touch and offer him your details.

1. **Set boundaries**

Stop trying to please everyone. You don't need to do that. Learn to say "no" when you're feeling overwhelmed. You can still be friendly, considerate, caring, courteous and respectful to others. Set clear boundaries and redefine what being nice to people means so that people don't walk all over you.

1. **De-clutter your life**

Getting rid of anything that is cluttering your life can be extremely healing. Deep down, we all are the hoarders of feelings. Start getting rid of the feeling and thoughts you don't need. Get rid of everything toxic from your life – physical, emotional and material (things that remind you of negative things). This will make room for the good.

1. **Stop living as tick boxes**

Stop stressing yourself by trying to live to the expectations of the society. Do not try to be tick boxes for others. You don't need to do anything for the sake of society. Getting married, having children, buying a big house –don't do any of these unless you want to do it. Figure out what you think success is and strive towards that. Doing things to just please others will not lead to happiness.

1. **Stop being scared**

Fear is the greatest obstacle to change. Most of it is just a game of our own mind. Real change needs you to stop letting your fears hold you back. Muster up courage to trade the path of success even if it's laid by obstacles. Figure out your blocks and remove them. Appreciate and reward yourself for being brave. You will love the new "fearless" self once you have overcome this hugely damaging negative emotion.

When you love yourself, you are more likely to be emotionally balanced and have a better sense of what is meant by "accepting yourself" – the good, the bad and everything in between. The most important decisions in your life depend on how much you understand yourself, your capabilities and limitations. And this comes from the commitment to love and accept yourself. Follow these key things to love yourself and be able to take the decisions that will take you to success!

SIX

THE THINGS YOU SHOULD STOP DOING TO YOURSELF

We are the greatest enemy of our own self. We cloud our minds with negativity and unimportant thoughts; we doubt ourselves and complicate our lives. We also hate ourselves, punish ourselves and then feel sorry for ourselves thinking that the "outside forces" are making our life a living hell. But dear friend...life is so beautiful! You're making your life a living hell on your own. It is you who is making living happily difficult for yourself.

Surely, some of you may have the things going really wrong. But, you can make your life beautiful by taking the corrective actions. And there are those - a big chunk of us - who are better off; yet make our own lives more difficult. Here are a few things you should stop doing to yourself to get away from the miserable situation you have found yourself in.

Stop running from your problems

There is no person in this world who is capable of handling every punch thrown at him. However, that doesn't mean you turn your back to the punches of life. Face them head on. It won't be easy. We are not made to solve every life problem instantly. In fact, we are made to get upset, hurt, stumble and even fall. But that's the whole purpose of living! Unless we face the problems, we can not learn from them. Turning our back to the problems makes us less capable at solving them over the course of time. And this ultimately molds us into the "incapable" person we become. Instead of running away from the problems, face them with confidence and think how you can solve them.

Stop lying to yourself

We can lie to anyone in the world, but we can not lie to ourselves. Your life can improve only if you are honest to yourself. You need to take risks and for that; you need to understand yourself. So, stop flattering yourself with false praises. Introspect to know and accept your weaknesses because that's the only way to win over them.

Stop putting your own needs on the backburner

The worst thing you can do to yourself is losing yourself in the process of loving someone else. Do not forget that you are special too. Yes, you should help others; but you do not have to stop looking after yourself. If there is ever a moment to follow your desires and passions, do what that matters to you.

Stop trying to be what you're not

The greatest challenge in life is to be yourself. We live in a world where everyone is trying to make you like everyone else and that may include your parents also. There will always be someone prettier than you, someone smarter than you and someone younger than you. But, they will never be you. Don't change yourself so that others like you. Be yourself and the people will appreciate you for what you are.

Stop trying to hold onto the past

Past is past, whether good or bad. Holding on to the past in any form can be detrimental for your future. You can't start a new chapter in your life if you keep re-reading your last one. Lamenting about past grief will push you into the dark dungeons where no ray of hope can reach you; while feeling high about your past success will just make you over-confident. It will make you lose your focus on the future goals. So, learn to let go the past, learn from your mistakes, feel more confident about your success and concentrate on your future goals.

Stop being scared about making mistakes

Doing something wrong is much more productive than doing nothing. Every story of success has several initial pages of failures and every failure is the step on which you can build your success. So, don't be afraid of doing mistakes. Instead, be prepared to go wrong sometimes and learn from them.

Stop berating yourself for old mistakes

You may have loved the wrong person or cried about the wrong things you did. But no matter how wrong the things went, one thing is for sure that such mistakes help us to find the things and the person that are right for us. We all make mistakes and have to struggle. But your mistakes and struggle make you what you are today. The mistakes have the power to shape your future. So, stop berating yourself for the old mistakes and see how you can get wiser from them.

Stop trying to buy happiness

Most of our desires are expensive. But the truth is; the things that actually satisfy us are totally free. Laughter, love and working on our passions, all of these do not ask for any fees. So, learn to be contented with these small happy moments in life rather than running behind monetary pleasure all the time.

Stop looking to others for happiness

If you do not feel happy from the inside, you will not be happy in any relationship with anyone. Create stability in your own life before you can share it with someone else. Look for happiness within you rather than expecting others to keep you happy.

Stop being idle

An empty mind is a devil's house. Keep yourself engaged with any activity. Do anything that you like such as drawing, listening to music or even reading a book. Go for a walk or hit the gym when you have time. Having plenty of time at your disposal will make your thoughts to go haywire allowing the devil to enter your mind and gnaw into your creativity.

Stop thinking that you're not ready

Nobody can be 100% ready when an opportunity knocks. Most great opportunities in life force us to step outside our comfort zones, which means you will not feel completely comfortable at first. So, stop waiting to feel at ease to start something new. Instead, challenge your abilities to take up what you may find difficult.

Stop getting involved in relationships for the wrong reasons

Choose your relationships wisely. There's no need to rush into any relationship. It's better to be alone than be in a bad company. If something is meant to be, it will happen with the right person and at the right time. Fall in love when you find the right person, not when you're lonely.

Stop rejecting new relationships just because the old ones didn't work

There is a purpose for why we meet every person in our life. Some will test you, some will harm you, some will teach you and some will use you. But most importantly, some will bring out the best in you. So, just because your last relationship didn't work doesn't mean you stop rejecting new relationships. Look at every new person you meet with an open mind.

Stop being jealous of others

Jealousy is an art of counting the blessings of others instead of your own. Jealousy can affect you negatively and take your focus away from your goals. It will force you to work on preventing others from achieving their goals rather than on the actions that will take you to your goals.

You can not go back and start a new beginning. But you can definitely start today and make a new ending. Begin this process of transformation by stopping to do the things that have been holding you back.

SEVEN
WHAT IS SELF-CONFIDENCE AND WHY IS IT NECESSARY?

Confidence is that step, which if you miss while climbing the ladder of success; you will not be able to reach the top. From a confident teacher whose lectures we never missed, to an inspiring speaker whose charismatic speech we love to hear, all self-confident people have the qualities that everyone admires. Most people struggle in life and are not able to achieve success because of the lack of this ingredient. And sadly, this leads to a vicious cycle: They fail because they lack self-confidence and the failure later reduces their confidence even further, which then reduces their chances of success even more. The good news is self-confidence can be learnt. Here's some information on what self-confidence means.

WHAT IS SELF-CONFIDENCE?

THERE ARE two main things contributing to self-confidence: self-esteem and self-efficacy.

We gain a sense of self-efficacy when we see ourselves mastering new skills and achieving goals pertaining to those skill areas. This gives you the confidence that if I learn and work hard in a particular area, I will succeed. This type of confidence is what leads people to persist in the face of setbacks and accept difficult challenges.

HOW MUCH CONFIDENT **do you seem to others?**

YOU CAN FAKE ANYTHING; but you can not fake confidence. It has to come from within. People judge you based on how confident you seem to them. Your level of confidence shows in several different ways: how you speak, your body language, what you say, your behavior and so on. Have a look at the following comparisons of behaviors and actions that are classified as confident versus behaviors associated with lack of self-confidence.

SELF-CONFIDENT *vs* **Low Self-Confidence**

- Doing what you believe to be right is confidence, whereas modifying your behavior based on what others think about it shows lack of confidence. A confident person has the courage to do what he thinks is right even if others criticize or mock them for it.

- A confident person is willing to take risks and go the extra mile in order to achieve better things in life. On the other hand, a person who lacks confidence prefers to stay in his comfort zone and avoids taking risks fearing failure.

- Admitting your mistakes and learning from them is a sign of self-confidence while trying to cover up mistakes and fix the problem before anyone can notice is a sign of low confidence.

- A confident person has the patience to wait for others to congratulate him on his accomplishments because he has faith in his capabilities and knows that the positive outcomes are the result of his hard work and determination. A person with low self-confidence often tries extolling his own virtues as often as possible and to as many people as possible as he is not sure of his own capabilities.

- When you are confident, you can accept compliments graciously. "Thanks, I worked very hard on this project. I'm pleased you recognize my efforts." On the contrary, a person who lacks confidence may dismiss the compliments offhandedly saying "Oh, that was nothing really. Anyone could have done it!"

AS YOU CAN SEE from these examples, the behaviors and actions that come up as a result of low self-confidence can be destructive. It has the danger of manifesting itself as negativity. Self-confident people are more assertive. They believe in their abilities and in living their life to the full. Learning to be confident can help you sail through the difficult times with ease.

EIGHT
HOW TO BOOST YOUR SELF-CONFIDENCE

Self-confidence is the most important ingredient in the recipe of success. Luckily, becoming more self-confident is readily achievable, as long as you have the determination and focus to carry things through. So here are some most powerful tips and habits that will help you in improving and maintaining your self-esteem and confidence even through the rough days.

SAY STOP **to your inner critic**

A GOOD WAY TO start with raising your confidence is to learn how to handle and replace the voice of your own inner critic. We all have an inner critic, which tells us only about the wrong things we have done. It pulls you down, makes you feel bad about yourself and tears apart your confidence. Though this inner critic may spur you on to do things to gain acceptance from the society, it may also drag your self-esteem down. This inner voice whispers destructive thoughts in your mind. Thoughts like for example:

- You are so sloppy and lazy, now get to work.
- You can never be good at any job. Someone will figure that out and show you the doors.
- You are uglier or worse than your partner/friend/co-worker.

YOU DON'T HAVE to accept everything that your inner critic says. There are ways to minimize this critical voice and replace it with helpful thoughts. This will help you to change how you perceive yourself. One way to do so is to say "Stop", "No, I am not listening to you" or "I know you are lying" whenever the critical voice pipes up in your mind. This will stop the train of negative thoughts driven by the inner critic. This will also make the voice of the inner critic weaker and at the same time, motivate you to take positive actions and raise your self-esteem. Once you have got used to the stop-word phrases, it will become a habit and your inner critic will pop up a lot less often. This will allow you to refocus your thoughts on something more constructive like planning your career, making strategies for business and so on. In the long run, this will help you to find better ways to motivate yourself.

USE **healthy motivation habits**

. . .

MOTIVATING yourself should be a continuous exercise. You should do it when you are facing a failure and also when you are basking in the glory of success. You need to motivate yourself to keep doing better; otherwise you are at the danger of getting commonplace. Keep reminding yourself of the benefits of staying motivated. A simple, yet, powerful way to keep your motivation up at all times is to note down the deeply felt benefits that you will get from following the new path or upon reaching a goal.

FOR EXAMPLE; if you are trying to lose weight, imagine yourself in the dress you have been itching to try since long; but are not able to do so owing to your unshapely curves. When you feel stuck at any point while working on something, remember the extra money that work will bring to you. Through that you will be able to travel with the love of your life and enjoy wonderful new things together. When your have prepared the list of benefits of your work or actions, put it somewhere where you can see it everyday like on your fridge or in your workspace.

REFOCUS ON DOING **what you really like to do**

WHEN YOU LIKE DOING something from your heart, then the motivation to do that thing comes pretty automatically. When you really want something in life, it becomes easier to push through any inner resistance you may feel. So when you think you are losing your motivation, ask yourself: "Am I doing what I really want to do?" If the answer is

"No", then you need to refocus and start working on that thing you want to do.

TAKE **frequent self-appreciation breaks**

THIS IS a simple and fun habit. Spend just 5 minutes on it every day for a month and see the huge difference it makes. Take a deep breath, feel the fresh air entering your body and ask yourself this question: "What are the 5 things I appreciate about myself?"

YOU WILL BE SURPRISED to see quite a number of things coming up in your mind to answer your question. You can make people laugh, you may have helped quite a few people, you are very thoughtful and caring for your family and so on. These things don't have to be big things. But they do make a lot of difference to others. And these small things in bits and pieces, when put together, make you a better person. Read this list again and again till a smile appears on your face and you start feeling good about yourself. Do this exercise every day. Over a period of time, it will not only build your self-esteem; but also turn your negative moods around and reload you with positive energy.

DO **the right thing**

DO those things that you deep down know are right. This

will raise and strengthen your self-esteem. It might be a very small thing like getting up from the couch and going to the gym. It may not be easy to do or even to know what the right thing is. But keep a focus on it as it can make a big difference for the results you get and for how you think about yourself.

REPLACE **the perfectionism**

PERFECTIONISM IS such a good habit to have. That's what many people think. However, this habit of trying to be perfect at everything can actually be destructive and may even lead to obsessive behavior. It can paralyze you from taking certain risks because you become so afraid of not living up to the standards you have set for yourself. And so you procrastinate and do not get the results you want. Beware, this can make your self-esteem sink. You must get rid of the thinking that anything less than perfection is failure. Learn to be satisfied with your achievements, small as well as big. Recognize every little success you have achieved rather than thinking about that little something you could not get.

HANDLE FAILURES **and mistakes in a positive way**

WHEN YOU GO OUTSIDE of your comfort zone and try to accomplish something that is truly meaningful, the chances are that you will stumble and fall along the way. But that is OK. In fact, you should pat yourself on your back for at least trying. Trying to do something meaningful is much better than not doing it at all even if you fail at it. People who do something truly meaningful and think out-of-box are the ones who achieve success. So do remember that. And when you stumble, try to find the upside to it. Focus on optimism and opportunities. Ask yourself: "What did I learn from this?" This will help you to change your viewpoint and make sure you do not hit the same bump further down the road.

BE KINDER **towards other people**

IT'S important to be kind and considerate towards others even when the destiny has not been the same to you. That's the test of your determination and perseverance. When you are kinder to others, you tend to treat yourself in a kinder way too. Just be there and listen to your friend when he wants to vent out his frustrations, encourage him when he is uncertain or unmotivated, hold up the door for the next person or take a few minutes to help someone out. The way you treat others will also change the way they treat you. And the kinder response you will get from others will help you feel confident and raise your self-esteem.

STOP FALLING **into the comparison trap**

WHEN YOU HAVE a tendency to compare your life with others' you have a destructive habit on your hands because you can never win against everyone. There will always be someone who is better than you at something. So, replace this habit with something better. Compare yourself with yourself. Look at how far you have come. Focus on your success and the positive results you have achieved in life. This will motivate you and increase your self-esteem.

THE ACTIONS you take or the things you do to build your self-confidence can lead you to success. Confidence is an essential component in almost every aspect of our lives. You can inspire others, including peers, your bosses, customers and friends, with your confidence. Confidence helps you to speak clearly while holding your head high. And you will be surprised to see how people are persuaded to take the actions you desired even though you may not know much of what you talked about. That's the magic of confidence! Hopefully, these tips will help you to break the vicious cycle of low confidence-failure-low confidence and take you to the top of the ladder of success.

NINE

HOW TO FIX RELATIONSHIP PROBLEMS THAT HINDER YOUR SUCCESS?

Conflicts are a normal part of any relationship. After all, two people can not be expected to agree on everything and at all times. Strained relationships are often the cause of unhappiness and dissatisfaction in life. Frequent conflicts over trifles can also reduce your self-confidence and also divert your attention from the more strategic issues resulting in failure to achieve your goals. Even in cases where relationship conflict is not the main cause of failure, the relationships are at the danger of falling apart when you are facing unfavorable circumstances due to other issues like loss of job. Whether strained relationships caused the failure or the failure strained the relationship, both ways, its important that you work towards bridging the emotional gap between you and your loved one so that your improved relationship gives you the support and courage to fight the problems in life with the better strength of joined hands.

What is a conflict?

- A conflict is more than mere disagreement. It is a situation in which both the parties perceive a

threat for agreeing to the views of the other (even though the threat is nonexistent).
- Since the conflicts involve perceived threats to our survival and well-being, they continue to fester until we face them and make efforts to resolve them.
- Our response to conflicts is based on our understanding of the situation and not on an objective review of the facts. And how we understand the situation is influenced by our culture, values and past life experiences.
- Conflicts trigger strong emotions. If you are not able to control your emotions, you will not be able to resolve the conflict successfully.
- Conflicts provide an opportunity for growth. When you are able to resolve a conflict, it builds trust and respect. You can feel secured knowing your relationship can survive disagreements and challenges.

The reason of conflicts in relationships

Understanding the reason of conflicts can help you dowse the flame of bitterness in relations. In most cases, the reason is differing needs. Conflict usually arises from differences, large as well as small. It occurs when people disagree over their motivations, values, perceptions, desires and ideas. These differences may appear trivial; but can trigger strong feelings. A deep personal need is usually at the core of the issue. These needs could be the desire to feel valued and respected, the need to feel safe and secure or a need for greater intimacy and closeness. In personal relationships, a lack of understanding about the needs of each other can create distance between them and result in arguments and break-ups. Here are some conflict resolution tricks that will help you strengthen the bond.

- **Understand the needs and expectations of others**

Everyone wants to be understood, supported and nurtured. But the ways by which these needs are expected to be met vary. Differing needs for feeling comfortable can create severe conflicts in our personal and professional relationships. Think about the need for continuity, stability and safety versus the need to explore and take risks. This kind of conflict is frequently seen between young children and their parents. The child's need is to explore; so climbing on the cliff meets his need. But the parents' need is to protect the child; so limiting the attempts of the child for the exploration becomes their need. And this conflict of needs becomes a bone of contention between them. Understanding and accepting the needs of both the parties play important roles in the long-term success of relationships.

- **Have a Thrill**

Sharing some exciting experiences together can boost the affection and attraction in a relationship. Doing something extreme like taking a skydiving lesson or as simple as watching a horror movie together can enhance the satisfaction in a relationship. The goal is to get your hearts beating together and create few memorable moments with the person you love. If possible, record the videos of the exciting moments or bring a camera along to capture the memories and replay them to re-live those magic moments whenever possible.

- **Use the Sense of Touch**

It has been proved that an affectionate touch has great healing powers. A hug, a kiss or even holding hands can trigger the body to produce a chemical called oxytocin. This substance invokes fond feelings and increases a sense of empathy between 2 people. The touch therapy works even when you are feeling depressed. A hug from someone or a pat on your back can help you feel reassured and give you the strength needed to face the challenge. Use this magical therapy whenever possible to improve your relations. Hold each others' hands, especially when an argument seems to be looming. This simple action can help you avoid resentment and keep the relationship afloat.

- **Fight Fair**

You can not escape from having arguments in relations. They are bound to appear from time to time. But you and your partner should have a pact to argue fairly to avoid the feeling of resentment. It is best to convey your feelings before they start piling up and turn into anger or frustration. When arguing; avoid raising your voice, abuse of any kind or threatening the relationship. Aim to be an attentive listener and wait for your turn to speak rather than trying to overpower your partner to make him listen to you. Don't think of the situation as a competition because whoever wins the argument; after all, it's your relation that will fail. So, be patient and understand the issue from your partner's perspective and try to put forward your point in a calm voice.

- **Stay Playful**

A playful approach can help reduce tension and keep your relationship lively. Create inside jokes with your love interest. Don't be afraid to make fun of yourself or goof around if you think that will work for your relationship. Partake in activities that stimulate your imaginations. For example; play a board game together. If you seem to be losing, just joke about it and laugh at yourself rather than ruining the mood with a defensive attitude. But, avoid any mean-spirited humor that pokes fun at your partner's flaws. Let your partner feel good about his or her win without being sarcastic.

- **Managing workplace conflicts**

In workplace, the differing needs are usually at the heart of bitter disputes resulting in lost jobs, broken deals and fewer profits. Recognizing the legitimacy of the conflicting needs and being willing to examine them in an environment of compassionate understanding can help open the pathways to team building, creative problem solving and improved relationships.

Learning to deal with relationship conflicts is crucial. When a conflict is mismanaged, it causes a lot of harm to a relationship. Handling your loved ones with respect and having a positive approach to the conflict provide an opportunity to strengthen the bond between two people. By learning the skills for conflict resolution, you will be able to keep your personal and professional relationships strong and growing, which will reflect on your self-esteem and confidence and also make way for your success.

TEN
GETTING RID OF PEER PRESSURE AND COMPARISONS

Our minds are vulnerable, especially during our teen years. We all have to go through a volatile phase in our life sometime or the other to gain status, security and social approval. An ill-intended comment of a friend or relative can make you conscious of your weaknesses and tarnish your self-image.

An inferiority complex is an unrealistic feeling of inadequacy that is usually caused by a supposed inferiority in any one sphere. Sometimes, it is marked by aggressive behavior meant to compensate for the perceived inferiority or to maintain one's superiority. In extreme cases, a feeling of inferiority can lead to depression. Before you learn to get rid of this negative baggage, let us first understand the signs of inferiority complex arising out of peer pressure.

Finding faults with others

People who don't feel good about themselves cannot appreciate the good in others. They find ways to find the imperfections in others. They have a habit of pulling people down for their own benefit. They fake relative superiority over others by condemning them in public. It is their way of compensating for the feeling of inadequacy they have for their self. They resort to destructive criticism to safeguard their fragile self-esteem.

Faking superiority

When a person is aware of his weaknesses and is reluctant to accept them, he starts to develop a fake feeling of superiority, which manifests itself in dogmatic opinions, boasts and views. He tries to maintain dominance in conversations and forces his views on others. This is a lethal feeling as he is aware of his inferiority; but adamantly puts on a mask to cover his complex and appear normal.

Flattery

People, who suffer from an inferiority complex, like to be complimented by others several times. They crave for attention from others. This kind of desperation also leads them to speak in a manner that prompts the other person to reciprocate with compliments. In most cases, however, they are suspicious of these compliments and fear that these compliments are an indirect way of reminding them of their flaws.

Jealousy and reluctance for competition

The thought of competition can be frightening for people with an inferiority complex. They avoid facing challenges especially when the opponent is far better equipped with skills. They are conscious that the competition will expose their flaws in public and will also prove the other person to be more competent. So, they avoid it so as to protect their image.

Comparison among peers is healthy, as long as it does not harm your self-esteem. If you are suffering from an inferiority complex, it's time you do something about it. Here is some advice on getting rid of this negative baggage so as to develop more self confidence.

Surround yourself with positive people

An inferiority complex can bring in negative thoughts of helplessness and worthlessness. The best way to overcome this state is to be associated with people who are positive in their approach and can motivate you to excel in life. Negative people are sinister in their approach and can make you feel more miserable. Get yourself away from such people at the earliest.

Read motivational books

Books are the best companions when you are lonely. Books can help you by channelizing your energy and thinking process towards better productivity and fill your mind with inspiring thoughts.

Improve yourself

When you are upset with your lack of confidence, with your intelligence or with certain aspect of your physique like weight or pimples - don't worry. These are the things that can be improved. Instead of feeling sorry for yourself, work towards overcoming these negative traits. Improving yourself will improve the way you perceive yourself. This will help you get rid of your inferiority complex.

Accept the things you can not change

There may be certain things that could be beyond human abilities to change. For example; some physical features, like your height, are largely determined by your genes. You can not increase your height beyond a certain age. If you compare yourself with someone else in terms of how short you are and how tall that person is, it's an unfair comparison. To feel inferior for something that was not the result of your own deeds is like blaming someone for the moon not seen on a new moon day! You do not have to feel bad for something that you have not done. Instead, focus on your positive traits. The tall person you are comparing yourself to is also not perfect. Every person is born with some good things and some flaws. So, accept what you can not change and move on to improve on your positivity.

Take up a hobby

The problem with having an inferiority complex is if you look at one flaw in your personality, then you generalize that and inflate its importance so much that you lose your confidence completely. The solution to this is to involve yourself in a hobby that you are good at so that you get your confidence from it. For instance, choose an activity or sport that you like and involve yourself in it. This gives you a dose of motivation every day and keeps you engaged with your good traits.

Love thyself

You will not feel the need to compare yourself with others if you are satisfied with your 'self'. Loving yourself is the first step to overcome peer pressure and inferiority complex. It sets the path for high self-esteem and stops you from wanting to be someone else.

Most people suffer from an inferiority complex due to comparisons with peers. Often, this fragile phase is accompanied by anxiety. Peer pressure and comparisons can also lower your self-esteem. Having a positive outlook on the comments of others and having determination to work on your weaknesses will help you get rid of the bad effects of peer pressure and concentrate on your goals. And one more thing; when you do achieve success, do not let others down by pointing to them how less successful they are when compared to you!

ELEVEN
TIME IS THE ESSENCE OF SUCCESS: LEARN TO MANAGE TIME

Do you wear a watch? We all do. And just in case you forget to wear it on any day; there's a clock on your cell phone, computer screen, dashboard and one hanging on the wall. Have you ever thought why every gadget, every room and every place in your life has a clock that tells you the time? The answer is simple. Time governs our activities and schedules and it is the last thing we would like to waste. So why is this time so precious? What does all this scheduling say about the value of time?

Time is our most valuable commodity

We humans are too obsessed with time simply because we have such limited amount of this commodity! We have only 24 hours in a day, just 7 days in a week (out of which we work for only 5 days) and so on. We can buy and sell any other commodity; but not time. We can change how we use it; but once we run out of it, there is no way to get it back. So we use watches and clocks to keep track of this precious and limited resource. Time management is one of the biggest determinants of success. The good news is that time management is a skill that can be learned and practiced.

Here are some proven strategies that can help you manage your time more effectively.

Start with making a list of activities

If your goal is to gain control over your time, you will first have to check what are the activities you have in hand and when each of it must be finished. Have a clear picture of the upcoming days, weeks and months to discover how much time is available for you to devote to study, work, family, recreation and other activities. This will make you the master of time, rather than its suffering slave!

Assess your time

Many people genuinely believe that they work a lot. Some even protest that they work all the time! But this is humanly impossible. The only way to realize for how many hours of your busy day you actually do anything meaningful is by having a personal assessment of your time and activities. The method requires you to keep track of everything you do for an entire week. Write down all your activities from the time you wake up to the time you fall asleep. Record every single detail.

At the end of the week, total the number of hours you have spent on studying, working, eating, traveling, shopping, exercising, talking on the phone, watching TV, smoking, being online and so on until you have a clear picture of where your time goes. If you find you are spending a lot of time on unproductive activities, try to balance your schedule. Start eliminating the time bandits by adjusting your habits and behaviors to gain better control over this precious resource.

Set your priorities

The objective of time management is to allocate your time based on your priorities so that you can achieve your objectives. If you want to be a ballet dancer or an Olympic swimmer, you will have to practice several hours a day for years. In the same way, if you want to excel in academics, you will have to devote a good amount of time to studying. By prioritizing, you will be able to increase the time devoted to the tasks that can take you to your objectives. This advance planning will also increase your awareness about your target and make sure you do not squander away your time meaninglessly.

Make a schedule

Once you have established your priorities, set up a schedule with respect to the tasks needed to fulfill them. A wide variety of tools are available that can help you schedule your activities like organizers, diaries, electronic tools and planners. Choose whatever seems convenient for you. Make sure that the system you select is something you are very comfortable with as you will be referring to it often. Then, set up your schedule in the planner. Start with marking all the fixed commitments like seminars and meetings. These are the givens that you cannot change. Add in the time needed for the activities you will do on your own like preparing for a presentation. Coincide these activities with the times of the day when you are most alert. In the last, mark in the other activities that are important; but lower in your priority list like exercising, socializing and recreational classes, which you can fit in when possible.

Use a calendar

In addition to a weekly planner, invest in a monthly wall calendar. Highlight the important deadlines and tasks so that they are in front of you as a reminder. This will keep you aware of the important dates and allow you to rearrange your plans if you are behind the planned schedule.

Use review cards

Keep some review cards that you can read over when

you are waiting for something else to happen like when waiting in a queue at the bank or traveling. You can also place these review cards at the locations from where you frequently pass, like your bathroom mirror, fridge door, etc. Frequent review is the key to remembering the information easily.

Plan activities biologically

Our body has a clock just like the clock on the wall. It is called the biological clock. Our body schedules its activities like sleep and eating based on the directions from this clock. Understand your bodily cycle and schedule your activities around this biological clock as much as possible. If you usually feel sleepy after lunch, then use this time to get your daily walk, instead of fighting to keep your eyes open for the work that needs careful attention.

Plan some down time

You are not a robot! You need some time to relax so that your mind and body are refreshed to start working again. Scheduling some down time will enable you to work more efficiently. Get enough sleep every day. A sleep-deprived person can not perform to his or her best. Schedule some time in a day or a week when you will keep all the work related thoughts aside and have some enjoyment. This will recharge your senses and give your body and mind the energy needed to utilize your time more effectively.

Reduce distractions

In today's age of social media, it's too easy to get distracted. Between watching the TV shows, casually checking Facebook, texting your friends, ... one can waste countless hours without doing anything. Work away from such distractions and turn off the technology when you are not using them! The time you save will add up in the long run!

To limit your distractions, follow the 50:10 rule: work for 50 minutes and then take a break for 10 minutes when you can allow yourself to check your social media, phone, etc.

Once the time is gone, it doesn't come back. So, learn to schedule and plan your activities according to the clock. Make your appointments and arrangements after calculating the time you have so that you don't miss out on important opportunities. Schedule your bed time and some vacation time also. Having your schedule in place will keep the stress off your mind and allow you to concentrate on the activity planned for the moment. Your undivided attention to the task will optimize your productivity and help you to attain your target.

TWELVE

HOW TO OVERCOME STRESS THAT PREVENTS YOU FROM ACHIEVING YOUR GOALS

Stress hits us all in life. Though a little amount of stress can be good — it keeps us motivated and focused— too much of it can grind our lives to a complete halt. When you're feeling stressed-out, your thinking becomes paralyzed making you incapable of doing anything meaningful. It is one of the greatest obstacles that can prevent you from achieving your goals.

Most people resort to unhealthy tactics to overcome stress. The unhealthy methods of managing stress can only worsen the situation. Turning to junk food, drugs or alcohol can turn one set of problems into another and balloon the problem out of your control. It's better to avoid such unhealthy coping mechanisms and find good ways to keep your stress in control. Here are a few tips and tricks to tame your anxiety and keep the stress monsters at bay.

Identify the source of stress

Stress management begins with identifying the source of stress. This may sound easy; but sometimes it can be difficult to locate the exact cause. Most people are not aware of the real causes of their stress. These sources are often hidden. They keep playing havoc at the back of our mind without making their presence felt. They aren't always obvious and hence, are usually overlooked by our own thoughts, behaviors and feelings. You may know that you're always stressed about the work deadlines. But, what you may not know is that it's your procrastination and not the actual job demand that is leading to the stress and anxiety.

To identify the true source of your stress, have a closer look at your attitude, habits and excuses. Do not consider the stress as a permanent phenomenon. Try to identify the time when the stress entered your mind and life. This will help you to pin point the event that lead to the stressful situation you are facing today. Stop considering stress as an unavoidable part of your personal life and career. Get rid of the attitude that says, "Things are always crazy around here". Do not blame the stress on other people. Until you accept the responsibility for your actions that have played a role in creating and maintaining the stress, it will be beyond your control to reduce it.

Understand how you are coping with the stress currently

Think about how you are currently managing the stress in your life. Are your strategies helpful or unproductive, healthy or unhealthy? Are you trying to manage the stress in a way that's only compounding the problem? Have a look at the unhealthy ways of coping with stress:

- Drinking too much
- Smoking
- Under-eating or overeating
- Spending too many hours in front of a computer or TV

- Withdrawing from friends and family
- Using drugs or pills to relax
- Sleeping too much
- Procrastinating
- Lashing out at others or resorting to physical violence

These coping strategies may help temporarily; but can cause more harm in the long run. These methods of managing stress do not contribute to your emotional and physical health. Hence, it's time to find the healthier ones.

Healthier ways of managing stress

As each of us responds to stress in a unique way, there's no "one size fits all" method to managing it. No single solution works for everyone and in every situation. So experiment with different strategies and techniques. Focus on the things that make you feel relaxed. There are several healthy ways to deal with a stressful situation, but they need a change. You can change the situation or modify your response to it. To decide which option to select, learn the four As: Avoid, Alter, Adapt and Accept. Here's how you can follow this 4-pronged strategy to cope with stress.

- **Stress management strategy #1: Avoid stress**

Though we can not remove all the stressors from our life, there are several of them, which can be eliminated, completely or partially. Indentify the stresses that you can avoid. Learn to say "no" to these stresses. In both your personal as well as professional life, taking up more than what you can handle is bound to cause stress. Hence, recognize your limitations and stick to them. Avoid people who consistently cause stress in your life. If you can't turn your back to the person, minimize the amount of time you spend with him or her. Take control of the environment. If traffic makes you nervous and causes frustration, take another route that may be longer; but is less-traveled. Avoid hot-button topics that you get upset over.

- **Stress management strategy #2: Alter or modify the situation**

When you can not avoid the stressor, modify it. Figure out the things you can do to change the situation so that the problem doesn't present itself again. This usually involves modifying the way you operate or communicate in your daily life. Learn to express your feelings instead of piling them up. If someone is affecting you negatively, communicate the same in a respectful way. Be willing to make compromises. When you expect someone else to change his or her behavior for you, be willing to do the same. If both of you are willing to bend a little; you'll stand a better chance of hitting on a common middle ground. Be assertive. Deal with the problems head-on rather than staying in a backseat in your own life.

- **Stress management strategy #3: Adapt to the situation**

When it's beyond human control to change the situation, change yourself. Adjust to the stressful situation and gain back your control by modifying your attitude and expectations. Reframe the problem and view the situation from a positive perspective. Instead of getting frustrated about a traffic jam, consider it as an opportunity to listen to your favorite music and enjoy some 'me' time. Adjust your standards. Trying to be perfect in everything is a very common source of preventable stress. Stop demanding perfection from yourself at all times. Be reasonable when setting standards for yourself and others and learn to accept what's "good enough."

- **Stress management strategy #4: Accept the situations that can not be changed**

Some stressors can not be avoided. You can't prevent or change some stressors like a national recession or a serious illness. In such a case, the best way to deal with the situation is to accept the things as they are. Acceptance can be difficult, but it will help you to deal with the life situation with better ease in the long run. Do not try to control the things that are beyond your control like the behavior of other people. Learn to forgive. We live in an imperfect world and people do make mistakes. Let go of the resentment and anger. Forgive others and move on to free yourself from the negative energy.

Sometimes, it may seem as if there's not much you can do to reduce the stress. There will never be more than 24 hours in a day, the bills will not stop coming and your family and career responsibilities will always remain demanding. But you can have more control on your life than you might think. The mere feeling that you're in control of your life can form a solid foundation for stress management. Managing stress using the methods given here will help you take charge of your emotions, thoughts, schedules and the way you deal with the seemingly huge problems and prevent this obstacle from taking you away from your objectives.

THIRTEEN
GOAL-SETTING: DEVELOPING A VISION FOR YOUR LIFE AND CAREER

Strained relations, lack of self-esteem and low self-confidence are all the hurdles that prevent you from having an accurate self-perception. This, in turn, also affects how you see yourself and may force you to dislike yourself. These are the obstacles that do not allow you to have a clear vision of your goals. Now that you have managed to overcome the hurdles in your path, get ready to develop the objectives you are trying to achieve. Have a clear image in your mind of who you want to be in the future? This vision is a "picture" of what you aspire to be. Articulating your vision statement is your next step that will eventually take you to success. Following are some tips that will help you create a vision statement that will inspire and energize you.

Carve out a chunk of time

Be prepared to devote time to your vision building exercise. Setting your vision statement should not be rushed. It's something that needs a lot of thinking and efforts and sometimes multiple revisions also. Be prepared for a few false starts before the things begin to get clearer and you start getting a grasp of your ideal future. Have the patience to revise your goals as many times as needed to get a clear picture that envisages a successful future.

Review your core work values

Our actions, goals and vision are based on the values and beliefs that have been instilled in us during our childhood. These core values impact our personal as well as professional life. Identify the values and actions that define you and set your goals keeping them in mind so that your vision is in line with your personality. If your goals are not in tune with your personality, there is a risk of your actions and efforts not running in tandem with the efforts needed to achieve the goals.

Suspend pragmatic thinking

Logical thinking is a part of success. We are always told to apply logic when trying to solve any problem. However, sometimes it's necessary to suspend this logical thinking as it does not allow us to break the barriers of pragmatic thoughts. When you are setting your goals, you need to think beyond your usual self. Applying logic while setting your objectives may turn on a negative thinking that will disallow you from following an untraded path and block you from thinking big.

Remember, setting objectives requires you to consider anything and everything possible to accomplish. Pragmatic thinking forces one to assume that the future is limited to what is happening today. Hence, to achieve success, it's important to delimit your thoughts and this can be made possible only by suspending your logical thinking.

Try visioning exercises

Take help of the visioning exercises to get your creative juices flowing. Think deeply about the questions given below and answer each of them as authentically as possible:

- What does success mean to you? Are you contended with the level of success you have achieved now or in the past? What kind of job will help you to achieve the success you are aiming at?
- What would you like to do today if you had unlimited cash reserves and if your all bills are paid automatically?
- What would your life be like if you are given the power to make it the way you want?
- What would you like your obituary to say about your life and accomplishments? What is the kind of impact you want to leave on the people you worked with?
- Who are the people you admire the most? What is it about them that you like?
- Which is the one activity that you love the most? Is it a part of your current life or profession? If not, how can you make it a part of your life?

Answering these questions will help you to understand your aspirations better. It will give a clear picture of what you want to be and where your capabilities lie. This will help you to take the right decisions for selecting a career that will allow you to do the things that you are good at and also like to do. This will maximize your chances of success and also keep you happier and satisfied.

Put it all together

Write your career vision using a concise paragraph or just one sentence. Write your vision statement with a short description of how you see yourself accomplishing it. Write everything in the present tense, as if you have already accomplished it. This will help create the right frame of mind rather than keeping your vision in the distant future.

Keep your vision visible

Once you have created your vision statement, plaster it in various places at your home or workplace and read it aloud as often as possible. This will remind you of your vision and motivate you to work harder to achieve success. Imagine yourself achieving the vision. Reinforcing the image of you in your vision, subconsciously and consciously, will help you to set the action steps that will lead you to your goals.

Review your career vision statement

Once you have set your vision statement, review it regularly. Your vision may change as you move closer to it. Review your vision statement and make adjustments to it as a part of your annual self-assessment exercise. Ask yourself the questions that helped you set this vision. If you find the answers to be different than the previous ones based on which you formed this vision statement, you may need serious rethinking. You may also need to revise your objectives if your previous vision is no longer appealing to you. This happens. You need not worry when you find yourself in this situation. This is possible when you have already achieved your goals or when the circumstances are no longer relevant to the objectives. Be prepared to change your vision rather than sticking to the old one that's no longer appealing. Have frequent reviews of your vision statement and check your progress against the yardsticks you have set. Make it a continuous process to fine tune your objectives.

Some more tips…

- Set realistic goals that you can achieve.

- Express your objectives positively, instead of framing them in terms of what you don't like or want.
- Be precise in setting dates and amounts so that you know where you stand currently.
- Set priorities to know which of your goals need more attention. This will also help you to avoid feeling overwhelmed for having too many goals.
- Break down your vision into smaller, achievable goals or tasks so that you get frequent opportunities to feel motivated once you have accomplished them.

These goal-setting techniques have been used by successful people in all fields. Setting clearly defined goals will help you to measure your progress and motivate you continuously to work towards the vision you have set for yourself. This will enable you to take the right actions to accomplish your goals and give you the confidence needed to overcome the challenges in life.

AFTERWORD

Every morning, we wake up with a hope of success. Each day, we try to move forward and step closer to our goals. Achieving success is like a journey; sometimes it can be easy and sometimes really tough. It can be short or very long. The road is often laid out by struggles and obstacles that make the journey challenging. However, having an eye on your goals will help you overcome every obstacle that tries to scare you away. Do not lose hope. Keep yourself healthy and happy. Do not get carried away by the disturbing thoughts of having to work harder. The harder you work; the more satisfied you will feel upon achieving the success.

Keep in mind the tips given here. Do not lose confidence in yourself. Have faith in your abilities. Polish your skills and learn new ones. Anything and everything that you learn will help you do better with the tasks in your life. Keep your self-esteem high. Love yourself. Accept yourself the way you are. Be aware of your strengths and strive to fight the weaknesses.

Use your time wisely. Plan the days, weeks and months ahead keeping in mind the tasks you want to complete in that period. Keep provision for some downtime and have a few days off for vacation. Keep yourself free from stresses. They will not allow you to attain your goals. Work around the stressors to get rid of them or alter them. Work on improving your relations also – both personal and professional - as a healthy relationship is vital for a happy and successful life. Do no allow undue peer pressure to take hold of your confidence.

Set clear goals. Understand yourself to know what you want to do or become in life. Be prepared to face challenges. Identify the factors that motivate you and increase your energy to go forward. Look for those that obstruct your journey and find ways to cope with them. These are the strategies that will help you conquer every difficult situation in life and take you to your destination point.

How do you think you will feel when you succeed? Satisfied? Happy? Confident? Or overconfident? Do not let overconfidence come in the way of your next goals once you have achieved the initial success. Be confident, satisfied and happy. This will take you higher and higher to the more difficult goals and give you a sense of fulfilment, which is the ultimate objective of a human life!

www.ingramcontent.com/pod-product-compliance
Lightning Source LLC
Chambersburg PA
CBHW052119110526
44592CB00013B/1678